I0410774

POTENTIAL TERRORIST THREATS: BORDER SECURITY CHALLENGES IN LATIN AMERICA AND THE CARIBBEAN

HEARING

BEFORE THE

SUBCOMMITTEE ON
THE WESTERN HEMISPHERE

OF THE

COMMITTEE ON FOREIGN AFFAIRS
HOUSE OF REPRESENTATIVES

ONE HUNDRED FOURTEENTH CONGRESS

SECOND SESSION

MARCH 22, 2016

Serial No. 114–155

Printed for the use of the Committee on Foreign Affairs

Available via the World Wide Web: http://www.foreignaffairs.house.gov/ or
http://www.gpo.gov/fdsys/

U.S. GOVERNMENT PUBLISHING OFFICE

99–553PDF   WASHINGTON : 2016

For sale by the Superintendent of Documents, U.S. Government Publishing Office
Internet: bookstore.gpo.gov Phone: toll free (866) 512–1800; DC area (202) 512–1800
Fax: (202) 512–2104   Mail: Stop IDCC, Washington, DC 20402–0001

COMMITTEE ON FOREIGN AFFAIRS

EDWARD R. ROYCE, California, *Chairman*

CHRISTOPHER H. SMITH, New Jersey
ILEANA ROS-LEHTINEN, Florida
DANA ROHRABACHER, California
STEVE CHABOT, Ohio
JOE WILSON, South Carolina
MICHAEL T. McCAUL, Texas
TED POE, Texas
MATT SALMON, Arizona
DARRELL E. ISSA, California
TOM MARINO, Pennsylvania
JEFF DUNCAN, South Carolina
MO BROOKS, Alabama
PAUL COOK, California
RANDY K. WEBER SR., Texas
SCOTT PERRY, Pennsylvania
RON DeSANTIS, Florida
MARK MEADOWS, North Carolina
TED S. YOHO, Florida
CURT CLAWSON, Florida
SCOTT DesJARLAIS, Tennessee
REID J. RIBBLE, Wisconsin
DAVID A. TROTT, Michigan
LEE M. ZELDIN, New York
DANIEL DONOVAN, New York

ELIOT L. ENGEL, New York
BRAD SHERMAN, California
GREGORY W. MEEKS, New York
ALBIO SIRES, New Jersey
GERALD E. CONNOLLY, Virginia
THEODORE E. DEUTCH, Florida
BRIAN HIGGINS, New York
KAREN BASS, California
WILLIAM KEATING, Massachusetts
DAVID CICILLINE, Rhode Island
ALAN GRAYSON, Florida
AMI BERA, California
ALAN S. LOWENTHAL, California
GRACE MENG, New York
LOIS FRANKEL, Florida
TULSI GABBARD, Hawaii
JOAQUIN CASTRO, Texas
ROBIN L. KELLY, Illinois
BRENDAN F. BOYLE, Pennsylvania

AMY PORTER, *Chief of Staff*   THOMAS SHEEHY, *Staff Director*
JASON STEINBAUM, *Democratic Staff Director*

———

SUBCOMMITTEE ON THE WESTERN HEMISPHERE

JEFF DUNCAN, South Carolina, *Chairman*

CHRISTOPHER H. SMITH, New Jersey
ILEANA ROS-LEHTINEN, Florida
MICHAEL T. McCAUL, Texas
MATT SALMON, Arizona
RON DeSANTIS, Florida
TED S. YOHO, Florida
DANIEL DONOVAN, New York

ALBIO SIRES, New Jersey
JOAQUIN CASTRO, Texas
ROBIN L. KELLY, Illinois
GREGORY W. MEEKS, New York
ALAN GRAYSON, Florida
ALAN S. LOWENTHAL, California

(II)

CONTENTS

POTENTIAL TERRORIST THREATS: BORDER SECURITY CHALLENGES IN LATIN AMERICA AND THE CARIBBEAN

TUESDAY, MARCH 22, 2016

House of Representatives,
Subcommittee on the Western Hemisphere,
Committee on Foreign Affairs,
Washington, DC.

The committee met, pursuant to notice, at 2 o'clock p.m., in room 2200 Rayburn House Office Building, Hon. Jeff Duncan (chairman of the subcommittee) presiding.

Mr. DUNCAN. A quorum being present, the subcommittee will come to order. We have an eight-vote series that will require the subcommittee to recess for about 45 minutes as soon as votes are called. I understand that Assistant Secretary Bersin has a hard stop at 4 o'clock, so we will return immediately after votes to conclude the opening portion of the hearing and to move to a classified setting. Following testimonies and members' questions, we will conclude there and we will conclude our time today.

So I am going to, in the essence of time, skip over my opening statement, but I want to start off with just saying a couple of things. First off, I am deeply saddened by the loss of life in Brussels today at the hands of evil men. I want to dedicate today's hearing to the victims of today's attacks and their families. I led my first congressional delegation trip to Brussels in 2014 to look exactly at foreign fighter flow, foreign fighter threat, and the ways that the U.S. and our European allies could better cooperate on homeland security issues. And only a day before my visit, an ISIS foreign fighter had returned to Brussels and shot up a Jewish museum killing four people before he tried to flee to Africa. So today's depraved acts in Brussels, following the Paris attack, demonstrate again that evil and evil men's intentions continue to rip apart the fabric of free Western societies through acts of terror and fear.

It brings to mind Winston Churchill's words. Let us learn our lessons. Never, never, never believe any war will be smooth and easy. Always remember, however, as sure as you are that you can easily win, that there would not be a war if the other man did not think he also had a chance. So we must show enemies that they have no chance of victory and we do that, in part, through strong defenses and secure borders.

So I want to start the hearing. We are going to jump right in and submit our opening statements for the record. The ranking member agrees with me, so I would just go ahead and recognize Mr. Gonzalez for his opening statement. You are recognized for 5 minutes.

STATEMENT OF MR. JUAN GONZALEZ, DEPUTY ASSISTANT SECRETARY, BUREAU OF WESTERN HEMISPHERE AFFAIRS, U.S. DEPARTMENT OF STATE

Mr. GONZALEZ. Thank you, Mr. Chairman, Mr. Ranking Member, and distinguished members of the committee. Thank you for the opportunity to testify before you on border security and vulnerabilities in Latin America and the Caribbean. It is an honor to be here with my colleague and friends from the Department of Homeland Security.

First, just to summarize my oral remarks, I wanted to first thank this committee in my capacity as Deputy Assistant Secretary of State for Central America and the Caribbean for its bipartisan support for our strategy in Central America. You allowed us to increase funding for Fiscal Year 2015 and supported the President's Fiscal Year 2016 request for $750 million, providing us with the tools to help these governments make a real difference on the ground. So thank you and I look forward to continue working with you on this.

Now effective border management in Latin America and the Caribbean is vital to our economic prosperity and national security. Throughout the hemisphere, we are working with governments to eliminate trade barriers, integrate electricity grids and energy markets, connect national infrastructures, and cement commercial relationships. As evidence, I offer that our trillion dollar trade relationship and over 3 million American jobs, supported by our economic relationship with Canada and Mexico, demonstrate what is possible when governments collaborate actively.

At the same time that we are using our border cooperation to promote prosperity, we are equally determined to use them to safeguard the homeland and to ensure safe, legal, and orderly migration to the United States. Border security was a focus of the recent Canada state visit. We always share travel information with Canada, including our respective no-fly lists. And the President and Prime Minister Trudeau used their meeting to discuss what more we can do to secure our borders while actively promoting commerce.

We are also working with Mexico on border enforcement at both its northern and southern border to regulate migration, combat smuggling, and target narco-traffickers and our counterterrorism cooperation with Mexico is excellent.

During his fourth visit to Mexico under this administration, Vice President Biden discussed border security with President Peña Nieto as he chaired at the same time the third meeting of the U.S.-Mexico High Level Economic Dialogue.

Border security has also been at the front and center in the Vice President's active engagement on Central America since 2014. During his latest meeting with Northern Triangle leaders here in Washington on February 24th, the three Presidents reaffirmed their commitment to continue awareness campaigns about the risks of undocumented migration, deepening the fight against human smuggling and trafficking, continued regional border security coordination, the strengthening of task forces and development of joint intelligence and border security facilities, and facilitate with the return, repatriation, and especially the reintegration of migrants who do not qualify for humanitarian protection in the United States.

Our efforts in the Caribbean are aimed at combating the drug trade and other transnational criminal threats and work in lock step with the U.S. Coast Guard, the Department of Defense, and Department of Homeland Security to support regional maritime and aerial domain awareness by improving radar coverage and information sharing between partner nations. Caribbean governments are using U.S.-provided equipment and training to identify threats and carry out interdiction operations. And the U.N. Office on Drugs and Crime Container Control Programme is establishing dedicated container profiling units to improve port security.

In South America, the Tri-Border Area of Brazil, Argentina, and Paraguay is a focus for regional law enforcement efforts, as you know from your recent congressional delegation. Governments in the region have long been concerned about arms and drug smuggling, document fraud, money laundering, trafficking in persons, and the manufacture and movement of contraband goods through the Tri-Border Area. We are working with all three governments on their efforts to improve border management and combat smuggling. We brought justice and police officials from Paraguay to regional conferences on money laundering conducted with the Department of Justice.

Mr. Chairman, to conclude, throughout our efforts in the hemisphere, U.S. strategy development and program design has been an active exercise of coordination between the Departments of State, Homeland Security, Justice, Commerce, USAID, and others. Indeed, funding from the Department of State and USAID supports a lot of the work of our partner agencies. At the same time, the expertise and experience of our DHS colleagues, as well as others in the departments and agencies, have helped us refine our approach and we continue to look for ways to maximize our coordination.

And I will close where I began, Mr. Chairman. The U.S. Congress is a vital partner to the administration and we look forward to engaging with you on our discussion today on border security and vulnerabilities in Latin America and the Caribbean. Thank you for holding this important hearing and I look forward to engaging in the discussion.

[The prepared statement of Mr. Gonzalez follows:]

**Testimony of Deputy Assistant Secretary of State Juan Gonzalez
Before the House Foreign Affairs Subcommittee on the Western Hemisphere
March 22, 2016**

Mr. Chairman, Mr. Ranking Member, distinguished members of the Committee, thank you for the opportunity to testify before you on "Border Security and Vulnerabilities in Latin America and the Caribbean." It is an honor to appear before you with my distinguished colleagues from the Department of Homeland Security (DHS).

Effective border management in Latin America and the Caribbean is a vital component of our economic prosperity and national security strategy in the Latin America and the Caribbean. Throughout the hemisphere, we are working with governments to eliminate trade barriers, integrate electricity grids and energy markets, connect national infrastructures, and cement commercial relationships. Our trillion-dollar trade relationship and the over three million American jobs supported by our economic relationship with Canada and Mexico bear testament to the benefits of collaboration between governments on border management.

Just as we promote the movement of goods and services, we are equally determined to safeguarding the homeland and to ensuring safe, legal, and orderly migration to the United States. From each of us today, you will hear about our whole-of-government efforts to collaborate with regional governments to face the significant and real threats of organized crime, drug trafficking, human smuggling, and terrorism. These include our major initiatives in Central America, Mexico, the Caribbean, and Colombia, as well as our bilateral and regional programs that bring governments together to facilitate information sharing and develop best practices around customs, border management, and document fraud. I will highlight but a few in my testimony.

As the President and Canadian Prime Minister Justin Trudeau highlighted during the recent State visit, the United States and Canada partner closely to address threats at the border and throughout our countries. Together, we have taken important steps to ensure the security of our countries, prevent criminal and terrorist actors from exploiting legitimate trade and travel, and expand North American perimeter security. We actively share traveler information developed joint protocols to exchange information on those who present a clear threat, including exchanging our respective "No-Fly" lists. Additionally, Canada is completing the last phase of a coordinated entry and exit information system to ensure the record of land and air entries into one country establishes an exit record from the other.

U.S.-Mexico cooperation on border management and migration issues is also excellent. Mexico is a strong partner with growing capabilities and a commitment to increasing efforts to regulate migration through Mexico. In his fourth visit to Mexico under this Administration, Vice President Joe Biden and Mexican President Enrique Peña Nieto discussed ways to strengthen border security, facilitate legitimate commerce and travel, and reduce the flow of undocumented migration. Mexico is working to safely return migrants and to build capacity to repatriate Central American migrants. Through the Merida Initiative, the United States and Mexico have forged a multi-faceted partnership to strengthen Mexican institutions and enhance their ability to respond to security needs.

Mexico continues to bolster law enforcement efforts in locations where organized criminal groups have the highest interaction with migrants, in particular at its southern border and along common routes toward the United States. We support these efforts with more than $130 million in fixed and mobile non-intrusive inspection equipment and small detection devices; canines to detect narcotics, explosives, weapons, and currency; and extensive training to Mexico's National Migration Institute in partnership with DHS. Mexico continues to increase the numbers of undocumented migrants it apprehends at its southern border and in the interior of Mexico.

On February 24, Vice President Biden also hosted Northern Triangle Presidents from El Salvador, Guatemala, and Honduras to review our joint efforts to address the region's security and development challenges. The three Presidents reaffirmed their commitment to continue awareness campaigns about the risks of undocumented migration to deter would-be migrants from making the dangerous journey north; deepen the fight against human smuggling and trafficking through the strengthening of the legal and institutional framework; continue regional border security coordination through the strengthening of task forces and the development of a joint intelligence and border security project; and facilitate the return, repatriation, and especially the reintegration of migrants who do not qualify for humanitarian protection in the United States. Additionally, in January, Secretary John Kerry announced plans to expand the Refugee Admission Program to vulnerable individuals from El Salvador, Guatemala, and Honduras to provide a safe alternative to the dangerous journey that many are taking at the hands of human smugglers.

Bipartisan support from the U.S. Congress has been indispensable to our Central America strategy. The $750 million Fiscal Year 2016 appropriation Congress provided will strengthen our ability to help regional governments tackle the underlying security, governance, and economic conditions driving migration from the region. Northern Triangle governments have committed a significant amount of their own resources to address these regional migration issues, but they cannot do it on their own. U.S. support in the way of training, technical assistance, mentoring, and equipment has produced such successes as "Operation Lucero," in September 2015, where law enforcement authorities in El Salvador, Guatemala, and Mexico arrested 36 individuals alleged to be smuggling hundreds of migrants each month from Central America and Mexico to the United States.

The Northern Triangle governments have also put in place their own travel requirements that prohibit minors from leaving their countries alone without permission from both parents. With U.S. support, the Northern Triangle governments are also improving their repatriation facilities and capacities along with expanding the services they provide to returned migrants.

We have also been working closely with immigration, law enforcement, and border officials in Central America to enhance their capacity to control their borders and ports of entry, including screening and processing special interest aliens. These capabilities help authorities capture, share, and analyze biometric information on migrants who cross their borders and focus attention on those who require extra scrutiny.

Our efforts in the Caribbean have been aimed at combating the drug trade and other transnational criminal threats and improving border security. We are supporting regional maritime and aerial domain awareness by improving radar coverage and information sharing between partner nations. Caribbean governments are using U.S. provided equipment and training to identify threats and carry out interdiction operations. The UN Office on Drugs and Crime (UNODC) Container Control Programme is establishing dedicated "container profiling units" to improve port security. We are providing equipment to help identify and inspect suspect containers. This assistance builds capacity to detect, identify and inspect high-risk containers.

In South America, the Tri-Border Area of Brazil, Argentina, and Paraguay is a focus for regional law enforcement efforts. Governments in the region have long been concerned about arms and drug smuggling, document fraud, money laundering, trafficking in persons, and the manufacture and movement of contraband goods through the Tri-Border Area. We are working with all three governments on their efforts to improve border management and combat smuggling. Through the International Law Enforcement Academy (ILEA) we are training police from Brazil. We brought justice and police officials from Paraguay to regional conferences on money laundering conducted with DOJ.

Throughout our efforts in the hemisphere, U.S. strategy development and program design is a function of active coordination between the Departments of State, DHS, Justice (DOJ), Commerce, the U.S. Agency for International Development (USAID), and others. Indeed, funding from the Department of State and USAID supports much of the work of our partner agencies, including the successful efforts of our partners at DHS Homeland Security Investigations. At the same time, the expertise and experience of our DHS colleagues, as well as other Departments and Agencies, have helped us refine our approach and we continue to look for ways to maximize our coordination.

The U.S. Congress is also a vital partner to the Administration in that regard, and we look forward to engaging with you on our discussion today on border security and vulnerabilities in Latin America and the Caribbean. Thank you again for holding this important hearing and I look forward to your questions.

———

Mr. DUNCAN. Thank you so much.
Secretary Bersin.

STATEMENT OF THE HONORABLE ALAN D. BERSIN, ASSISTANT SECRETARY FOR INTERNATIONAL AFFAIRS AND CHIEF DIPLOMATIC OFFICER, U.S. DEPARTMENT OF HOMELAND SECURITY

Mr. BERSIN. Mr. Chairman, Ranking Member Sires, Mr. Yoho, thank you for the opportunity to appear before you once again, particularly in the company of my distinguished colleagues, Misters Gonzalez and Kubiak.

I wanted to express our gratitude, certainly mine, for the comments you made with regard to the events in Brussels. I think in retrospect it will be seen in terms of European security and the effect on its borders as a game changer, building on what happened in Paris in January.

I was at a meeting of the European Institute today in which people were reacting to the events in Brussels and I thought it would be useful in the context of the hearing that you and your staff have structured, to offer some comments that I offered there. Because in fact, Europe is in the midst of a confluence of migration, refugees, asylum seekers, and terrorists. And in fact, it has set the European market on its back in the eurozone and the Schengen zone and it is placed them at great risk.

And in looking at the way in which the European nations have reacted to the crisis that they face with respect to border security, we begin to see them shutting down their individual borders, renouncing the Schengen zone, and generally hunkering down in ways that were reminiscent of the way in which we handled border security in the immediate aftermath of 9/11 when we shut down our airports. We shut down our seaports. We actually backed traffic south into Mexico and north into Canada by 10 to 20 miles as we looked at every trunk and we processed every passenger.

And I thought, reflected, for our European colleagues today how different our border security looks. To be sure, we are not seamless and we are not perfect and we are in a mode of continuous improvement as the discussion in the SCIF will undoubtedly focus on some of the issues that we should not take up in public session. But think about the difference in the way in which we handle border security from 15 years ago.

We used to see borders as lines on a map, the line that separated us from Mexico or Canada. And in fact, we now come to see because, in fact, we have learned that homeland security is intrinsically transnational. That is to say there is hardly an event that affects us inside our homeland that does not have a cause or effect that originates outside the homeland.

So we start to look at border security in terms of not just in lines, but in flows. And in the global world that makes a lot of sense in terms of the constant movement of migrants, capital labor, electrons, goods, and people, constantly back and forth across the line.

So we have come to see the fact that our ports of entry, the 327 airports, seaports, and land ports, are not the first line of defense, but rather they are the last line of defense. And what we have to do is secure the flow of goods and people toward the border lines, toward our homeland, as far away from them as possible, and as early in time before the arrival at the border. And we have implemented that as the testimony of my colleagues and I today will again document, but with which the chairman and Ranking Member Yoho are familiar.

The second thing that was pointed out, so that, in fact, don't move away from your—don't just hunker down at your border line, but manage the flows. And think our testimony will show that we do that.

Second is don't fragment your border agencies. I know that in the 1990s there were at each of our ports of entry there were three separate port managers, one from Treasury, for Customs; one for Justice, for Immigration; and one from Agriculture for agricultural inspection. As a result of the creation of DHS, we have actually created an integrated set of missions that will improve over time as the Defense Department has to actually perform a single border security function effectively.

Third, we recognize that you cannot stop everything. We are looking for a needle in a haystack, because in fact, 97, 98 or more percent of the passing of people and goods are perfectly lawful and legitimate. And when we look for the needle in the haystack, we have developed means and methods of doing it, but we recognize that it is based on risk management and making assessments and managing our borders, not seamlessly, but with the data that we have and the intelligence that we can garner.

Lastly, we have learned that we cannot do this alone, that we have to do it in partnership not only inside the government, among the agencies of the United States Government, but also with foreign partners. And a lot of our border security today with regard to migration, as well as drugs, as well as intellectual property protection, as well as counterterrorist activity depends on the partnerships that we have created with our foreign partners.

As Mr. Gonzalez indicated, we have just embarked on a massive effort in partnership with Central America. It will not solve the problem overnight. These problems are in the making over generations, but we have actually taken, and I take it during the course of the hearing, we can explore some of the departures that bode well and work well than the situation we have seen.

With regard to the Caribbean, we have similar efforts of partnership and I hope to be able to take those up, Mr. Chairman, in the course of the questions and answers.

So in conclusion, the challenge of our times is that the future is not what it used to be, as the French poet said. But we have changed the way in which we manage the border and I look forward to answering your questions so we can explore where there have been improvements and where there remains work to be done. Thank you, sir.

[The prepared statement of Mr. Bersin follows:]

WRITTEN TESTIMONY

OF

ALAN D. BERSIN

**ASSISTANT SECRETARY FOR INTERNATIONAL AFFAIRS AND
CHIEF DIPLOMATIC OFFICER
OFFICE OF POLICY
U.S. DEPARTMENT OF HOMELAND SECURITY**

BEFORE

**THE HOUSE COMMITTEE ON FOREIGN AFFAIRS
SUBCOMMITTEE ON THE WESTERN HEMISPHERE**

ON

**"Potential Terrorist Threats: Border Security Challenges in Latin America and the
Caribbean"**

March 22, 2016

Introduction

Good morning Chairman Duncan, Ranking Member Sires, and distinguished Members of the Subcommittee. Thank you for inviting the Department of Homeland Security (DHS) to testify on furthering U.S. security by ensuring cooperation and information sharing in the Western Hemisphere. Secretary Johnson and I appreciate this Subcommittee's interest in this important matter.

Overview

We have reached an important time for North America, with the region emerging as an economic powerhouse, consisting of a half billion people and 25 percent of global gross domestic product. Trilateral commerce between the U.S., Canada, and Mexico has increased 265 percent since the start of the North America Free Trade Agreement. If we are to remain competitive globally, however, we must adopt a whole of North America approach to perimeter security as well as trade facilitation. With respect to security, the focus must shift from an exclusive focus on land border lines, extending east and west, but also must recognize the reality of global flows of people and goods north and south in our hemisphere and increasingly adopt a continental perimeter approach to our security.

The lens of North American integration provides a viable framework for Mexico, Canada, and the United States to jointly address shared continental and perimeter security responsibility as well as the problems of violent crime and economic stagnation that exist in Central America's Northern Triangle countries. Thus, robust coordination among Canada, the United States, and Mexico through the North American Leaders Summit and other mechanisms is vital to Central America's efforts to promote development and security. As part of our whole-of-government approach, DHS continues to build our risk-based approach with our North American partners to address the challenges present in the region. Through information sharing efforts and law enforcement collaboration, we aim to address threats at the earliest point possible before they reach our borders to strengthen the shared security of our countries.

DHS Engagement with Canada toward Achieving Perimeter Security

The United States and Canada have a long tradition of working together to promote security and facilitate trade and travel across our borders, ensuring that they remain open to legitimate trade and travel and closed to terrorists, criminals, and illegal or unauthorized goods. The *Beyond the Border Declaration: A Shared Vision for Perimeter Security and Economic Competitiveness* and its accompanying *Action Plan*, announced by President Obama and then-Prime Minister Harper in 2011, has deepened and institutionalized this cooperation within, at, and away from the shared border. To that end, during Prime Minister Trudeau's recent State visit to Washington, D.C., he and President Obama announced our countries have jointly developed protocols to exchange information on those who present a clear threat, including exchanging our respective "No-Fly" lists, with appropriate protections for the handling and dissemination of such information and processes to correct inaccurate information.

Through the Beyond the Border initiative, the United States and Canada are enhancing perimeter security by systematically checking the other's visa and immigration databases for immigration and border related purposes, including visa and refugee resettlement applications, for third country nationals. As a result of this sharing, the United States and Canada have identified individuals with immigration violations, criminal concerns, and national security concerns who otherwise might have been missed. In 2013, Canada began checking biographic information on visa and refugee applicants to Canada against United States holdings through the Department of State's (State) Consular Lookout and Support System database, which contains records based on derogatory information related to fraud, criminality and terrorism.

In 2015, the United States deployed new technology significantly improving its sharing of biometric information with Immigration, Refugees and Citizenship Canada and the Canadian Border Services Agency in order to counter identity fraud, strengthen identity management and provide valuable information to inform respective admissibility determinations. Beginning in May 2015, this capability allowed Canada to vet the fingerprints of applicants for visas to Canada as well as refugees and those seeking asylum in Canada against the DHS Automated Biometric Identification System (IDENT) for the first time. The IDENT system contains millions of records of immigration violators, deported felons, as well as records from the Department of Defense and the Terrorist Screening Center. As a result of this information sharing, DHS was able to provide Canada advanced warning of likely illicit travelers. Through this information sharing, Canada has succeeded in rejecting a number of fraudulent applications that would have likely been approved. Canada is providing similar access to its biometric data to the United States.

On March 10, 2016, the Government of Canada publicly assured the United States it will complete the last phase of a coordinated entry and exit information system to all travelers, so the record of land and air entries into one country establishes an exit record from the other. Currently, this information is exchanged on third country nationals and permanent Canadian and U.S. residents. In 2015, the United States and Canada securely shared entry records on approximately 8.7 million travelers, with a cumulative total of 17.8 million since June 30th, 2013.

DHS Engagement with Mexico and the U.S. Southwest Border
Over the past few years, DHS has worked with its partners in the Federal Government to respond comprehensively to a substantial increase in the number of unaccompanied children (UC), who are some of the most vulnerable individuals to interact with our immigration system, apprehended at the U.S.-Mexican border. According to U.S. Customs and Border Protection (CBP), the number of UCs from all countries apprehended at the U.S.-Mexican border climbed from more than 24,000 in fiscal year 2012 to nearly 39,000 in fiscal year 2013, and to nearly 69,000 in fiscal year 2014. Total apprehensions on the U.S. Southwest Border followed this trend, with 356,873 apprehended in fiscal year 2012, 414,397 in fiscal year 2013, and 479,371 in fiscal year 2014. Yet the total number of apprehensions on the U.S. Southwest Border fell to 331,333 in fiscal year 2015, and UC apprehensions for fiscal year 2015 also decreased to just under 40,000, in large part due to the response by DHS, our excellent coordination with the government of Mexico on regional migration issues, as well as our interagency and international partners to prepare for the seasonal increase in migrants that normally begins in the winter and increases each spring. In response, CBP deployed additional Border Patrol Agents to high-traffic areas, augmented operations in South Texas with Mobile Response Teams, and redirected support from other Border Patrol sectors including through remote interviewing technology. CBP also increased surveillance capabilities by adding tethered aerostats (long-range radars) and other technology, along with additional aircraft. During the first three months of fiscal year 2016, DHS saw an increase in the number of UC and family units apprehended along the Southwest border, at a time of year when border crossings traditionally decrease. Although the number of UCs apprehended at our border has dropped from 6,775 in December 2015 to 3,111 in January 2016, and 3,113 in February, CBP will sustain its heightened border

security efforts, along with the humanitarian aspects of its responsibilities. DHS will continue to closely monitor these trends and coordinate across the whole of government to ensure an effective response to any changes in migration flows.

DHS plays a comprehensive role in migration management and security engagement in the region, focusing on border security, narcotics smuggling, human trafficking and smuggling, anti-gang initiatives, and police reforms across a wide range of law enforcement and police activities. Similarly, DHS is pursuing efforts to promote trade, travel, and commerce through trade facilitation, port infrastructure assistance, and information sharing. DHS currently has attachés and advisors working closely with their counterparts in Mexico and all of the Central American countries except for Nicaragua and Belize, although these two countries are covered by Panama and Guatemala attachés, respectively. DHS personnel in the region facilitate and support training and capacity building efforts as well as the systematic sharing of information.

In Mexico, DHS continues to deepen cooperation with Mexico counterparts to address human smuggling, to include working with our Mexican partners to coordinate enforcement efforts on the U.S.-Mexican border. DHS and Mexico are also working to shut down the criminal groups and illegal networks that exploit vulnerable migrants in the Mexico-Guatemala border region. Through information sharing, exchange of best practices, and training, DHS and our Mexican counterparts are working together to improve security for both countries. DHS will continue working with the State Department in support of the Merida Initiative, the longstanding partnership between the United States and Mexico, to fight transnational organized crime and associated violence while furthering respect for human rights and the rule of law.

In the context of Mexico, DHS has partnered with the Department of Defense's U.S. Northern Command and State's Bureau of International Narcotics and Law Enforcement Affairs on an information sharing initiative with the Government of Mexico called the Biometric Data Sharing Program with Mexico (BDSP/M). The purpose of this program is to develop and implement an automated biometrics solution for the Government of Mexico's (GOM) National Institute of Migration that will assist in the identification of Third Country Nationals traveling through Mexico. The BDSP/M initiative will support the exchange of biometric information between the GOM and the United States to improve regional security along the Southwest border, better identify transnational criminal threats, and bolster U.S national security through the identification of special interest aliens (SIA).

Regional Flows

The migration of Cuban nationals to the United States has also dramatically increased in recent years. The increase is likely due to the interaction of migration policies set by the Governments of the United States and Cuba, misperceptions about what the 2015 re-establishment of diplomatic relations will mean for migration policies, and the relatively weak state of the Cuban economy. Far larger numbers of Cuban migrants have attempted to enter the United States by land in recent years than have attempted entry by sea, where they are generally interdicted and returned to Cuba. So far in fiscal year 2016, encounters with Cuban migrants at land ports of entry have increased 84.3% over the same period in fiscal year 2015. In fiscal year 2015, 24,374 Cubans arrived at U.S. land ports of entry in fiscal year 2014, almost entirely along the U.S. Southwest border. In fiscal year 2015, the figure was 43,334. A growing number of Cuban nationals arrive at the U.S. Southwest border after traveling through Central America and Mexico. Cuban nationals fly to Ecuador before traveling through Colombia, Central America, and Mexico to arrive at the United States. The GOM temporarily detains large numbers of

Cuban migrants who arrive at its border without authorization before paroling them for a short period of time. Most Cuban nationals depart Mexico rather than claim asylum. Mexican Immigration officials do not have the authority to detain Cubans with valid Mexican visas or those who travel on Spanish passports. Although there are more land arrivals than in previous years than sea arrivals, Cuban maritime migration flow exceeded the five year average by 111%.

In addition to Central American migrants apprehended on the U.S. Southwest border, DHS apprehensions of special interest aliens, or extra-hemispheric migrants, have increased in recent years. This population consists of unauthorized migrants who arrive in the United States from, or are citizens of, several Asian, Middle Eastern, and African countries. While many citizens of these countries migrate for economic reasons or because they are fleeing persecution in their home countries, this group may include migrants who are affiliated with foreign terrorist organizations, intelligence agencies, and organized criminal syndicates. Human smuggling organizations will fly migrants from outside of the hemisphere to airports in the Western Hemisphere, particularly Brazil and Ecuador. Smugglers then exploit visa free travel arrangements and corrupt officials to smuggle migrants to northern South America and Central America before crossing into Mexico via a mixture of air, land, and maritime routes. These smugglers are often part of the same networks that move economic migrants from Central America and Mexico north to the U.S.

Virtually all of these migrants are trying to reach the U.S.-Mexico Border. Many migrants from outside the Western Hemisphere, or extra-hemispheric migrants, are apprehended by Mexican immigration authorities in the Mexican Southern border region. After encountering these individuals, and often due to a lack of consular response from the consulates or embassies in-country, Mexican authorities are often forced to release the extra-hemispheric migrants who cannot be deported, many of whom continue their smuggler-led journey to the United States. Central American countries, led by Panama, also detain migrants from outside the hemisphere, but are stymied in their efforts to return these migrants to their home countries due to a combination of factors, to include lack of detention space, lack of diplomatic representation (to issue travel documents), and lack of funding to support asylum hearings and removal operations via commercial aircraft. Still, DHS is working with interagency partners and the Governments of Central America and Mexico to increase law enforcement operations and information sharing regimes to detect, deter, and dismantle human smuggling operations moving extra-hemispheric migrants through the region and identify threats as far as possible from the U.S. Southwest border.

On January 4, 2016, Secretary Johnson announced a number of ongoing and new actions that will address recent trends and improve southwest border security, including increasing border security, cracking down on criminal smugglers, and expanding cooperation with international partners. All of these measures, in concert with actions undertaken by our interagency and regional partners, will make it that much more difficult for extra-hemispheric migrants to move unimpeded into and through Central America and Mexico and approach the U.S. border.

DHS Engagement with Central America

To shape and focus the U.S. Government's response to the challenges in Central America, the Obama Administration created the Strategy for U.S. Engagement in Central America, focused on three major objectives: prosperity, governance, and security. State is currently leading the effort to match funding ($750 million appropriated in fiscal year 2016) for programs in support of the broader strategy, with specific programs implemented via the Central America Regional Security Initiative (CARSI), the primary U.S. implementation structure for security assistance in the region. Through CARSI, partner nations work with State, DHS, and other departments and agencies to strengthen institutions, counter the effects of organized crime, and uphold the rule of law. More specifically, DHS collaborates with State and our regional partners to build capacity for border security, information sharing, and deterring transnational crime to address the region's most pressing security needs.

Through direct engagement with affected countries, increased operations targeting regional human smuggling networks, and foreign assistance to the region, the United States continues to direct its efforts towards improving the security and economic situation in Central America. Through CARSI and other funding initiatives, the United States will continue to expand successful programs to make short to medium-term sustainable impacts and reduce levels of crime and violence, build the capacity of law enforcement and rule of law institutions, and support prevention programs for youth and in communities at-risk of crime and violence. The viability and stability of Central America have profound national security and economic implications for the United States. If economic prospects remain poor and rates of violent crime remain high in Central America, the region will remain a source of instability for Mexico and ultimately the United States in the form of illegal migration and even more entrenched organized crime in the Western Hemisphere, including in the United States. To the extent that these problems constitute grounds for individuals to seek asylum or other international humanitarian protections, the United States will continue to provide appropriate protections consistent with our laws and international treaties.

DHS continues to utilize its excellent bilateral partnerships with our counterparts in the Honduran, Salvadoran, and Guatemalan Governments to enhance the quick, efficient, and safe repatriation of children and families who are apprehended in the United States, who are subject to a final order of removal issued by an immigration judge, and who have no outstanding appeal or claim for asylum or other humanitarian relief under our laws. To provide participating nations with criminal history information in advance of an undocumented migrant's removal from the United States, U.S. Immigration and Customs Enforcement (ICE) uses the Criminal History Information Sharing (CHIS) program. DHS has CHIS agreements with our counterparts in the Governments of El Salvador, Guatemala, and Honduras.

To build capacity for anti-smuggling investigations, DHS, with State funding, is planning to expand the Transnational Criminal Investigative Units (TCIU), which are sponsored by ICE in Honduras, Guatemala, El Salvador, and Panama. Comprised of foreign law enforcement personnel, TCIUs facilitate information exchange, rapid bilateral investigation, and ultimately enhance the host country's ability to investigate and prosecute individuals involved in violations within the ICE investigative purview. Partner nation authorities in Central America, including immigration services and border police, collect biometrics in cooperation with the TCIUs and through ICE's Biometric Identification Transnational Migration Alert Program (BITMAP). The host country owns the biometric data and shares the information with ICE for intelligence and screening.

To strengthen air, land, and maritime border security efforts in the region, DHS, acting primarily through CBP, is providing assistance and capacity-building at and between ports of entry. DHS plans to expand border-focused vetted units, such as the Special Tactics Operations Group or *Grupo de Operaciones Especiales Tacticas* (GOET) in Honduras, to El Salvador and Guatemala. Through these vetted units, funded primarily by State, CBP provides training and capacity building to foreign counterparts, empowering them to identify, disrupt, and deter criminal organizations engaging in illicit cross-border activities in the region. In the maritime environment, the U.S. Coast Guard (USCG) performed a comprehensive naval assessment for the Government of El Salvador in fiscal year 2015 and plans to complete assessments for the Governments of Guatemala and Honduras in the near future. These assessments identify gaps in organizational structure and create a road map of potential areas where the USCG can provide capacity-building and training.

DHS will also support increased passenger and cargo information sharing via programs designed to collect and verify information through U.S. databases and help reveal transnational criminal organization smuggling routes. By pursuing efforts to expand Joint Security Programs and Advanced Passenger Information Sharing in Central America, DHS will augment the ability of host country law enforcement and migration officials to identify and respond to illicit trade and travel occurring at major transit hubs, primarily at the international commercial airports.

In my engagement with our Central American partners, I have been impressed and encouraged by the political will demonstrated by each country, which is a critical component to our success. Salvadoran law enforcement leaders have described the need to build investigative capacity within the national police, with a particular focus on building capacity on the border. In Guatemala, President Jimmy Morales outlined his security and immigration priorities for Secretary Johnson during their February meeting, emphasizing that his administration will prioritize aviation passenger information sharing systems and build border security capacity in the air, land, and maritime environments. Senior officials in Honduras have outlined their goal to increase capacity of domestic police units, particularly investigative capabilities, to crack down on crime and violence. The Government of Honduras also expressed a strong interest in pursuing efforts to improve airport security and migration control. These efforts are but a few examples of how the governments of Central America are taking ownership of these challenges.

One important step for the Northern Triangle governments was creating a strategic vision through the "Plan of the Alliance for Prosperity in the Northern Triangle: A Road Map" which was created by the three Central American countries themselves with support from the Inter-American Development Bank. This plan emphasizes the importance of regional economic integration through stronger transportation, communications, customs, and border linkages. In support of this Plan, the Northern Triangle governments are undertaking ambitious reforms and allocating over USD $2.6 billion from their national budgets in 2016. Following their February 24, 2016 meeting, Vice President Biden and the presidents of El Salvador, Guatemala, and Honduras issued a joint communique in support of the Plan, agreeing to take numerous actions to augment current efforts to combat transnational crime, improve border security, cooperate on migration management, and promote economic growth, among other initiatives.

DHS Engagement with South America

Elsewhere in the region, we've made great strides in collaborating with partner governments in South America to prevent the entry of terrorists, terrorist weapons, and their components into the United States, as well as reduce regional threats presented by transnational criminal organizations. To this end, DHS components have deployed nearly 40 full-time employees with regional responsibilities in five countries in South America, including Argentina, Brazil, Colombia, Ecuador, and Peru, who enhance engagement in a range of areas. DHS, in coordination with U.S. interagency partners, collaborates closely with South American governments to share information and build capacities to enhance security.

To support South American partner countries' investigative capabilities and enhance law enforcement information sharing, DHS, through ICE, engages with foreign law enforcement to combat human smuggling and terrorist finance networks. For example, under the Biometric Identification Transnational Migration Alert Program (BITMAP), DHS provides training and equipment to build partner countries' ability to collect biometric and biographic data on suspect individuals. BITMAP enrollments provide U.S. law enforcement and intelligence agencies information on foreign partners' law enforcement and border encounters of special interest aliens, gang members, and other persons of interest who may pose a potential national security concern to the United States. BITMAP is currently operational in Colombia and, pending funding, will expand to other countries in the region in 2016. DHS also works to combat trade-based money laundering, in which transnational criminal organizations (TCO) move and launder illicit proceeds disguised as legitimate trade, through Trade Transparency Units (TTUs). TTUs currently operate in in Argentina, Colombia, Ecuador, Paraguay, and Peru, and we are working to expand to Brazil, Chile, and Uruguay in the coming months.

To enhance border security and help prevent illicit travel to the United States, DHS, through CBP, partners with South American countries to enhance the security at and between ports of entry through training, capacity building, and information sharing programs. For example, CBP is working to partner with countries across South America to support capabilities to detect individuals that may require additional screening when they enter and leave the country. CBP, in collaboration with ICE and other U.S. government agencies and using some funding from State, also provides training on fraudulent document detection, with recent courses in Brazil. To support secure air travel to the United States, DHS through TSA, works with partner countries with last point of departure flights to the United States to perform airport assessments and inspections, as well as provide training to enhance international airport security measures. Recent trainings include collaborating with FBI to provide airport police authorities a seminar on Advanced Improvised Explosive Device Post-Blast in Argentina, and baggage handling system training in Chile.

To enhance maritime security, the USCG partners closely with partners in South America to include Colombia, Peru, Ecuador, Suriname, and Venezuela to counter the flow of narcotics and counter transnational criminal organizations. Over the last five years, Coast Guard assets operating in the offshore regions of the transit zone have removed more than 450 metric tons of cocaine with a wholesale value of nearly $15 billion, removing a major source of funding for these criminal organizations. At maritime ports, CBP, through the Container Security Initiative, partners with Argentina, Brazil, and Colombia to address the threat to border security and global trade posed by the potential terrorist use of a maritime container to deliver a weapon to the United States.

In areas that are hotspots for illicit activity, such as the tri-border region where Brazil, Argentina, and Paraguay intersect, we provide in-depth, focused trainings aimed at countering illicit flows. For example, in 2015 ICE provided Cross Border Financial Investigations Training to the countries of the tri-border areas to increase the participants' ability to investigate transnational illicit financial and smuggling schemes used by terrorists, foreign fighters, and other TCOs. In 2016, we are seeking to enhance our efforts in this region, including exploring options for additional personnel and training that could be supported by State funding.

DHS also provides specialized trainings in advance of large events. DHS, in coordination with the U.S. interagency, worked closely with Brazil in the run up to the 2015 World Cup to support security efforts across multiple cities in Brazil. Likewise, in advance of the 2016 Olympics in Rio de Janeiro, DHS is working closely with Brazilian counterparts on measures to address a range of Olympic-related security issues, including training on fraudulent documents, and a workshop to increase Brazil's ability to halt the proliferation of weapons of mass destruction and its related commodities, and the trafficking of destabilizing conventional arms.

Conclusion

We appreciate the support Congress has provided to improve security at our borders and ports of entry. With that support, we have made significant progress. There are now increased personnel, technology, and infrastructure on our borders, more than ever before. As we work to increase border security, however, we must continue to collaborate with our regional partners and look beyond our borders to identify and interdict threats at the earliest possible point, before they reach our borders. To achieve this goal, we are sharing more information with these partners in a manner that preserves the privacy protection laws and policies of each country; we are working in a joint capacity to counter transnational criminal organizations, human and drug smugglers, and those who traffic in persons; and we are building greater security and integrity into our shared systems of trade and travel. We will continue to engage with our foreign and interagency partners to extend our security beyond our borders and address threats as far from the homeland as possible.

Thank you for the opportunity to testify today, for your continued support of the Department, and for your attention to this important issue. I would be pleased to answer any questions at this time.

Mr. DUNCAN. Thank you, sir.

Mr. Kubiak.

STATEMENT OF MR. LEV KUBIAK, ASSISTANT DIRECTOR FOR INTERNATIONAL OPERATIONS, U.S. IMMIGRATION AND CUSTOMS ENFORCEMENT, U.S. DEPARTMENT OF HOMELAND SECURITY

Mr. KUBIAK. In the immediate wake of the tragic attacks today in Belgium, I am strengthened by the fact that our international law enforcement collaboration and our effectiveness grows stronger every day. In my more than 20 years as a Federal law enforcement officer, ICE has never had greater capability to partner internationally to protect our nation.

Over 400 ICE personnel are assigned to 62 offices in 46 countries and each year we augment that staff with hundreds of agents and analysts on temporary detail. As today's attacks demonstrate, the threat continues to evolve and challenge our law enforcement response, but I am confident our strong global partnerships build our capability to identify criminals, terrorists, and those networks that support their actions.

As the goal of the hearing is today to address Western Hemisphere affairs, I will focus specifically on that area, but the accomplishments and programs that will be discussed today are representative of our efforts globally.

In the Western Hemisphere, ICE has 23 offices in 9 countries, staffed by about 111 people who work on capacity building and exchange of best practices with our law enforcement counterparts and then operationalize those capabilities through joint investigations covering a full range of ICE's broad investigative authorities and work with our partner nations to repatriate their nationals.

We are, at our core, a border law enforcement agency, and partner with our foreign law enforcement counterparts, Immigration and Customs officers around the world, to investigate transnational criminal organizations operating globally. Thanks to the additional appropriated funds from Congress in Fiscal Year 2015 and continued funding support from the Department of State and the Department of Defense, we have expanded critically important programs like the Transnational Criminal Investigative Units, our Biometric Identification Transnational Migration Alert Program, and the Trade Transparency Units.

We continue to build our capacity and the capacity of our host country counterparts through training programs such as our Cross Border Financial Investigations Program, and our Strategic Trade Control Workshops. We put these programs and training to work through ambitious international and multilateral whole of U.S. Government joint investigative enforcement operations such as Operation Citadel.

ICE's Transnational Criminal Investigative Units investigate all forms of illicit trade, travel, and finance. TCIUs are comprised of foreign law enforcement officials, customs officers, immigration officers, and prosecutors, who undergo a strict vetting process and complete a prerequisite 3-week training course at our Federal law enforcement training center in Glynco, Georgia. Once trained, the TCIU members work collaboratively with our attaché personnel to address significant joint law enforcement threats throughout the hemisphere. Through this program, ICE attachés share law enforcement intelligence, conduct joint investigations, and assist in prosecutions of transnational criminal organizations both in the host country and in the United States.

TCIUs are currently operational in nine countries and comprise more than 250 vetted foreign trained law enforcement officers who in 2015 alone, Fiscal Year 2015 alone, disrupted and dismantled criminal organizations through the arrest of almost 700 suspects, the seizure of nearly 17,000 pounds of cocaine, the seizure of more than $6.7 million in illicit cash, and $13 million worth of counterfeit merchandise, not to mention numerous firearms, ammunition, vehicles, and vessels.

One of ICE's highest priorities in the region is investigating human smuggling and trafficking. The Human Smuggling Cell serves as the U.S. Government's coordination center for all human smuggling investigations and through it ICE and CBP together harness DHS's unique access to immigration border and financial data to advance efforts to counter these organizations. The cell provides intelligence coordination and supports U.S. and foreign investigations to more effectively address the specific regional threat.

For the last 4 consecutive years, as an example, ICE led Operation Citadel, a regional, multilateral, and multi-agency effort to address our transnational criminal organization operations, but with the specific focus on human smuggling. This operation coordinated attachés and TCIUs in the region and combined partner national capacity building, training, and real-time intelligence, interdiction and investigative operations at international seaports, airports, land borders, and in the interior of those countries.

In Fiscal Year 2015, Operation Citadel dismantled several large transnational human smuggling organizations. Most significantly, one investigation coordinated collaborative investigations at the same time in Honduras, El Salvador, Guatemala, Mexico, and the United States, dismantling a prolific transnational criminal organization operating throughout Central America and throughout the hemisphere. As a result, 14 separate human smuggling routes were identified and disrupted, including routes used by smugglers to move third country nationals from the Eastern Hemisphere through the Western Hemisphere and into the United States across the southwest border. In total, Citadel's 2015 results included 210 arrests, the recovery of 51 unaccompanied minors, the seizure of $2.1 million in currency, over 2100 biometric collections or enrollments and the initiation of 68 new and on-going investigations.

There is much work still to do and the need to continue to strengthen international partnerships through training and joint operations, but ICE is fully engaged in addressing current and future threats. I am confident that we will continue to build upon this momentum and generate additional considerable operational achievements as we move forward. Thank you for the opportunity to answer your questions.

[The prepared statement of Mr. Kubiak follows:]

U.S. Immigration and Customs Enforcement

STATEMENT

OF

LEV J. KUBIAK

ASSISTANT DIRECTOR FOR INTERNATIONAL OPERATIONS
HOMELAND SECURITY INVESTIGATIONS
U.S. IMMIGRATION AND CUSTOMS ENFORCEMENT
DEPARTMENT OF HOMELAND SECURITY

REGARDING A HEARING ON

"Potential Terrorists Threats: Border Security
Challenges in Latin America and the Caribbean"

BEFORE THE

U.S. HOUSE OF REPRESENTATIVES
COMMITTEE ON FOREIGN AFFAIRS
SUBCOMMITTEE ON THE WESTERN HEMISPHERE

Tuesday, March 22, 2016
2200 Rayburn House Office Building

Introduction

Chairman Duncan, Ranking Member Sires, and distinguished Members of the Subcommittee:

Thank you for the opportunity to discuss the international engagement efforts of U.S. Immigration and Customs Enforcement (ICE). I am honored to provide an overview of our international operations and highlight some successes and challenges I believe we currently face.

I would like to briefly outline the structure of ICE to help you understand our mission and responsibilities. ICE is divided into three operational components: Enforcement and Removal Operations (ERO), Homeland Security Investigations (HSI), and the Office of the Principal Legal Adviser (OPLA). The role of ERO is to identify, apprehend, and ultimately remove individuals who are unlawfully in the United States in accordance with law and policy. HSI investigates transnational crime and conducts a wide range of domestic and international criminal investigations arising from the illegal movement of people and merchandise into, within, and out of the United States, often in coordination with other federal agencies. OPLA provides specialized legal advice within ICE and is the exclusive legal representative for the United States in exclusion, deportation, and removal proceedings before the Executive Office for Immigration Review at the U.S. Department of Justice.

ICE enforces an extremely broad set of federal laws and regulations with jurisdiction over the investigation of crimes with a nexus to U.S. borders and ports of entry. We focus our broad investigative authority on three operational priorities – border security, public safety, and counterterrorism/national security. ICE investigates offenses that stem from its traditional customs and immigration authorities; weapons smuggling and illegal exports of defense-related materiel and technology; war crimes and human rights violations; drug and contraband smuggling; financial crimes; cybercrimes and child exploitation; human trafficking and human smuggling; commercial fraud and intellectual property violations; transnational gangs; and document and benefit fraud, to name a few.

I would like to broadly discuss ICE's international operations and note some successes we recently achieved with our foreign partners. ICE's international operations serve two very important functions. First, our overseas agents and officers further the domestic law enforcement operations of our field offices in the United States. Second, they work to build capacity and share information with our foreign partners to stop threats before they reach our nation's borders. ICE deploys approximately 250 Special Agents, 11 Deportation Officers, and 176 support staff to 62 offices in 46 countries. The agency works with foreign counterparts to mitigate threats to public safety and national security through investigative activity.

In Fiscal Year (FY) 2015, ICE collaborated with international counterparts to arrest over 2,400 suspects abroad, and to seize $21 million in criminal proceeds, 400 firearms, 193,000 pounds of drugs, and $37 million worth of counterfeit merchandise. These statistics demonstrate ICE's efforts to attack foreign transnational criminal organizations (TCOs) at their root.

Transnational Criminal Investigative Units

The effectiveness of ICE overseas stems from the quality relationships we have with our foreign law enforcement counterparts. The relationships we build with foreign authorities are fundamental to attacking TCOs. ICE is particularly proud of the formalized relationships it has established with numerous foreign law enforcement partners through its Transnational Criminal Investigative Units (TCIUs).

ICE established TCIUs and International Task Forces to enhance transnational efforts against all forms of illicit trafficking with a particular focus on human smuggling. TCIUs are comprised of foreign law enforcement officials, customs officers, immigration officers, and prosecutors who undergo a strict vetting process and complete a prerequisite three-week International Task Force Agent Training (ITAT) course at the Federal Law Enforcement Training Center (FLETC). Upon completion of training, TCIU members work together with ICE to investigate significant threats.

TCIUs facilitate seamless information exchanges between ICE special agents and their host nation partners. These units provide a mutual benefit to the United States and the host nation. The Attachés ICE has deployed worldwide – including 23 locations in the Western Hemisphere – share intelligence, conduct joint operations, and assist in prosecutions of transnational criminal organizations both in-country and through the U.S. judicial system. TCIUs also enhance the host country's independent ability to target criminal activities that threaten the stability and national security of the region and pose continuing threats to the security of the United States.

Currently, there are nine units in the TCIU program with more than 250 foreign law enforcement officers. During FY 2015, our TCIUs arrested approximately 694 suspects, seized nearly 17,000 pounds of cocaine, more than $6.7 million in cash, nearly $13 million worth of counterfeit merchandise, and numerous firearms, vehicles, and vessels from TCOs.

With additional funding provided by Congress in 2015, ICE expanded TCIUs in El Salvador, Guatemala, Honduras, the Dominican Republic, and Colombia, and reestablished an additional TCIU in Mexico. The 2015 expansion included the graduation of 120 personnel at the three-week ITAT training course.

Human Smuggling Investigations

Investigating human smuggling and human trafficking organizations are two of ICE's highest priorities. As part of our overarching efforts to combat human smuggling, ICE leads two interagency initiatives: the Human Smuggling Cell and Operation Citadel. The Human Smuggling Cell (HSC) created an innovative model that synthesizes the four pillar disciplines of Investigation, Interdiction, Intelligence, and International engagement from DHS component agencies in investigations involving criminal networks. The HSC harnesses DHS's unique access to immigration, border, and financial data to develop information on individuals or organizations involved in human smuggling. It also serves as the coordination center for all ICE investigative operations to combat human smuggling organizations, and develops and distributes intelligence products.

In summer 2015, ICE led an interagency effort focused on human smuggling in Colombia, Panama, Guatemala, Honduras, and El Salvador under Operation Citadel. This operation, coordinated with TCIUs in the region, focused on partner nation capacity building and training with real-time intelligence, interdiction, and investigative operations at international seaports, airports, land borders, and other locations. Furthermore, Operation Citadel's operational and intelligence efforts supported our domestic investigations and the dismantlement of several large-scale transnational criminal organizations involved in human smuggling.

In 2015, Operation Citadel investigative efforts resulted in 210 criminal arrests, the recovery of 51 unaccompanied minors, $2,078,988 in seized currency, 2,133 biometric enrollments, and the initiation of 68 additional investigations. In addition to the ICE personnel, the 90-day investigative operation included U.S. Customs and Border Protection, the U.S. Coast Guard, the U.S. Drug Enforcement Administration, the U.S. Department of Justice, the U.S.

Department of Defense, and the U.S. Department of State playing a pivotal role to bolster host nation law enforcement, customs, and immigration enforcement capabilities.

Operation Lucero, another initiative under Operation Citadel, was a multinational investigation involving the unified efforts of four countries targeting a prolific TCO operating in Central America. Through the dismantlement of this TCO, 14 separate human smuggling routes were disrupted. Some of these human smugglers were responsible for moving third-country nationals from the Eastern Hemisphere through South and Central America to the Southwest Border. Therefore, ICE is leveraging increased information sharing and coordination to connect nodes of transnational crime through the DHS Human Smuggling Cell, as well as other international information hubs for intelligence and investigations such as EUROPOL and INTERPOL.

Counterterrorism and Counter-Proliferation Investigations

One of Secretary Johnson's top priorities is counterterrorism. At ICE, we seek to leverage our expertise and investigative methodologies to counter criminal and terrorist organizations. Both sets of bad actors seek to exploit legitimate U.S. trade, travel, and financial systems in furtherance of their financial or ideological objectives.

Within ICE, our goal is to prevent terrorist attacks against the United States before they materialize by ensuring that our various investigative programs, and domestic and international field offices, collaborate with the Intelligence Community and with federal, state, local, tribal, and international law enforcement partners. ICE is the second-largest contributor of federal task force agents to the Federal Bureau of Investigation's Joint Terrorism Task Forces (second only to the FBI itself), which rely on our investigative expertise and broad enforcement authorities.

Repatriation Efforts, Fugitives and Transiting Criminals, and Human Rights Violators

In addition to Special Agents overseas, ICE deploys Deportation Liaison Officers (DLOs) assigned to ICE Attaché offices who provide the necessary expertise to ensure the expeditious removal of aliens ordered removed from the United States. In addition, these officers conduct a significant level of foreign government liaison, assist in negotiating bilateral agreements on repatriation, and facilitate the issuance of identity documents in order to obtain the travel documents required to remove aliens from the United States. These officers liaise with foreign agencies and INTERPOL, and help obtain country clearances for ICE officers escorting aliens during removal missions. These officers also provide additional subject matter expertise to U.S. Mission personnel in the region concerning ICE's immigration and removal policies.

To enhance this mission, ICE is in the process of expanding its DLO footprint in ICE Attaché offices. Currently, officers are assigned to Thailand, China, Germany, Guatemala, Jamaica, Mexico, South Africa, Italy, El Salvador, the Dominican Republic, Honduras, Morocco, Brazil, the Netherlands, and EUROPOL. ICE will soon have personnel assigned in Austria, Egypt, and India.

ICE also works to locate foreign fugitives within the United States who are wanted for serious crimes committed abroad. ICE's DLOs are embedded both at INTERPOL and EUROPOL to identify criminals who have entered or are seeking to enter the United States or those who pose a public safety threat. Through ICE's Fugitive Alien Removal Initiative, we arrested an agency record – 345 foreign fugitives – within the United States in 2015. Partnering with INTERPOL and the U.S. Marshals Service, ICE conducted Project Red last year, which resulted in the arrest of 27 foreign fugitives wanted for various crimes including murder, kidnaping, and rape.

Finally, ICE personnel seek to locate, investigate, and remove human rights violators wanted for war crimes in their home countries. During Operation No Safe Haven I in 2014, ICE arrested 21 human rights violators. In Operation No Safe Haven II in 2015, ICE arrested 50 human rights violators. These at-large immigration enforcement efforts are directed by ICE's National Fugitive Operations Program, in coordination with HSI's Human Rights Violators and War Crimes Unit and the Human Rights Law Section of ICE's Office of the Principal Legal Advisor. Planning these operations also includes close coordination with our foreign government counterparts directly, including both INTERPOL and EUROPOL.

Conclusion

I am grateful for the opportunity to appear before you today and for your continued support of ICE and its law enforcement mission. I am confident that we will continue to build upon the momentum we have generated as a result of our considerable operational achievements around the world. ICE remains committed to working with this subcommittee to forge a strong and productive relationship going forward to help prevent and combat threats to our nation.

I would be pleased to answer any questions.

Mr. DUNCAN. Thank you. We will move into the question portion of the hearing and we will try to get through as much of the question portion as we can. When we break for votes, we are just going to end the portion of the committee hearing here. When we come back for votes, we will go straight to the SCIF, so I would ask the panelists to head on down to the SCIF when we leave for votes.

Mr. Gonzalez, following the Paris attack in November, there were press reports that indicated that the EU was considering tighter and systematic ID checks. Let me back up. Press reports and other reports surfaced that a Syrian individual, under investigation for participating in the attacks, had traveled to Brazil, Ecuador, and Colombia in July before bribing a Colombian official to leave the country. INTERPOL stated in November that the estimated 25,000 foreign terrorist combatants thought to be operating across the globe, only 5,600 have been identified by law enforcement agents.

So what can you tell me about the individual that may have traveled to Colombia and Ecuador and Brazil and him leaving the country? And I would also like for you to talk about the fact that we have a lot of folks from Syria and other places traveling the tri-border region on falsified or fake documents, exchanging those documents, and then transiting Latin America either to come here or to go in other places.

We just traveled, and we heard from the Paraguayans, and this continues to be the case. We saw the five Syrians that were apprehended in Honduras. So we know folks are traveling to this area. We know one of the Paris attackers possibly did. I would like for you to talk about that briefly, if you can.

Mr. GONZALEZ. Thank you, Mr. Chairman. First, thank you for taking that trip because I know this is an initiative you have been active on and it is something I know our whole government is actively devoting resources and time into. On this particular case, sir, we looked into, we heard the same reports. We looked into it and we had nothing to actually corroborate that it was somebody that was associated with the Paris attacks. In fact, what we did find was that it may have been a woman that was there fleeing violence from Syria. But it is something that we will continue to actually look into given the seriousness of the case and we can expand on this in the classified setting definitely.

Now with regard to the tri-border region, it is a place as you saw when you visited Ciudad del Este, that it is a place that does not have active border controls and it is incredibly concerning. We actually talk about perhaps issues that you have actually been very active on as well around Hezbollah. What we have found is that it is a place that illegal actors will use actively for financing, right? So that is definitely obvious.

What we have not been able to find is whether it is actually organized or whether it has actually been used as a stopping off point for any sort of organized attack or any sort of terrorist activity. However, it is a source of migration as the migration patterns throughout South America are incredibly complicated.

And the way that we would approach this, Mr. Chairman, is because we are in March, I am going to use the March Madness analogies. We are using man-on-man defense. As the Assistant Secretary Alan Bersin said, it is a needle in a haystack and we are actually actively looking for individuals that might pose a threat. And then on Central America and the Caribbean where I have played a more active role, we are playing zone defense where what we have been doing is investing resources to make sure that there is a presence of the state and that the rule of law is something that is being advanced. And that helps us whether it is migration, whether it is trafficking in persons, whether it is narco-traffickers. If you are actually working to support the governments of the northern triangle, the southern triangle and other parts in the Caribbean as well, and on the maritime, on the aviation, on border controls, something that we partner with DHS on, but also more importantly not just regarding the physical border as the area where we would focus, but with the judicial sector, strengthening police, and actually working to address crime and violence, we have actually seen amazing results. And in fact, we have had a couple of operations recently where we have been able to intercept special interests, aliens from different parts of the world, and of course, getting these countries to defend against undocumented migration.

I will say, sir, just my last point on this is that the majority of individuals that are traveling, be they from special interest alien countries or other places, we found the large majority of these individuals are actually fleeing violence from other parts of the world, but of course, we have to be very vigilant and we are looking at those individuals that might actually pose a threat and when we do, we actively work with these governments to respond.

Mr. DUNCAN. Thank you for that. And we saw very clearly that there are no border controls between Brazil and Paraguay. In fact, in Ciudad del Este it was wide open. An armed guard or two, but that is about it. We learned from the Paraguayans that there is no border control north of there anyway. In fact, a county road dissects the border and so when you are driving down the road, you might be in Brazil, you might be in Paraguay. So I guess I appreciate State and DHS working very well with the Paraguayans on counter-narcotics and counterterrorism efforts and I want to continue that.

So if we have episodes of say these five Syrians that were apprehended in Honduras and I think those were just the ones we know about that were caught, Secretary Bersin, you talked about a secure border. I agree that at our border checkpoints where we are pulling agriculture out to inspect it, we are trying to identify those coming across the border and at the border checkpoints, absolutely we are doing it a lot better than we ever have.

My concern on our southern border is all the areas that we are not patrolling, we are not fencing, we are not apprehending anyone. We are actually allowing interior enforcement to have a lead role in that. But then the administration is actually relaxed with interior enforcement, as well as policies of the administration I hope change in the next administration. But if someone can transit through Latin America through the tri-border region, hoping to do nefarious aims in the United States, then they could get to Mexico, just like the unaccompanied children or all the migrant workers that come into this country enter our southern border, without going through a border checkpoint that you talk about.

So I would like for you to talk a little bit about what the agency is doing on not the border checkpoints, not in Laredo or Nogales, I am talking about all those areas between the two. And whatever you can tell us in that because I will tell you this, my constituents are concerned that the soft underbelly of this nation is our southern border that is unsecured. If you can speak to that.

Mr. BERSIN. Mr. Chairman, so remembering our last exchange, we have a different set of experiences. I remember when this border was absolutely out of control when I became the U.S. Attorney, the so-called Border Czar in the 1990s, we were arresting one million, a million two, a million four unlawful migrants to the United States every year. That was an era when we had 3,000 border patrol agents, no cameras, no technology, and as a result of a bipartisan effort of President Clinton, President Bush, and President Obama, we invested $18 billion a year. And I simply disagree with the notion that there has been no difference in our southwest border. And we have 22,000 agents, 19,000 of whom are on the southern border.

So we have a difference of view of the relative state of the border. And I just think we should agree that no one claimed that we are ever going to seal this border like the Berlin Wall tried to seal people from leaving West Berlin, but no one should claim that it is a seamless border. That is to say that it is not susceptible to smuggling of people, but I can assure you with the number of apprehensions down at a 70-year low, at a time when we have 10 times the number of agents that I remember being on that border, the border is not what it used to be.

But let me take up the——

Mr. DUNCAN. Let me just speak to one comment you have made. If I am playing a football game, I can affect the score by not scoring. Apprehensions are down. I agree with you. But the border patrol people I talk to say the apprehensions are down because the administration wants them to be down.

I still think that we have people cross our border and we can disagree, but you can affect the score two ways. I yield back to you.

Mr. BERSIN. I have talked to some of those border patrol union officials over the 20 years I have been involved in border patrol and respectfully, you should look at the axe that there is to grind there. The fact is that it is a disservice to the men and women of the United States Border Patrol, sir, to claim that they are not doing their job on the border. They do. But let us leave that argument for another day. I think I understand your point.

But I would like to take up the five Syrians because I think they actually demonstrate good points and bad points of our contemporary situation. So on November 17 of 2015, five Syrians were encountered in Tegucigalpa, Honduras in Toncontin. They had arrived on a flight from Costa Rica and they presented photo altered Greek passports. Records checks indicated that the Greek passports had been reported stolen from Athens, Greece, and they were interviewed by HSI Transnational Criminal Investigative Unit agents stationed in Honduras, the TCI Units that Mr. Kubiak referred to. And the Syrians indicated that they were en route to the United States. They were placed in Honduran jails for 17 days and they were eventually released because of local laws that limited the amount of time that you could hold someone based on the administrative violation and the local asylum laws.

Subjects then proceeded by bus to Guatemala and on March 20th of 2016, four of the subjects were encountered at Laredo, Texas and they requested asylum. They were interviewed, processed, and transported by the border patrol and then by ERO to the Rio Grande Detention Center and are currently detained pending outcome of their asylum claims.

So here are the good points. We are doing a lot of work beyond the border with foreign partners to actually identify threats, particularly when they come from so-called special interest areas. But we did not have the capacity to take any action to either assist the Hondurans to continue to detain and then to transport people because of lack of authority. People then got to the border and claimed asylum. And as you know, because of the lack of resources provided to the Immigration Courts, those hearings will not take place in an expedited time so that we can take action.

But by the same token, they were not released simply to go into the country because—not because we had discovered any facts about any terrorist ties that they have because, in fact, they were fully vetted, but they were held because, in fact, we do not want to risk any danger from this particular population at this particular time.

So I think the case is actually a good indicator of progress that we have made, but an enormous amount of work we have to do, both to assist our foreign partners to develop border control capacities, but also frankly, to mend our immigration processes here at home.

Mr. DUNCAN. Thank you for that. I am going to turn to the ranking member.

Mr. SIRES. Thank you, Chairman. I just want to say the chairman put together a great codel, which was very informative for me. We certainly learned a lot about especially border crossing in some of these areas that have nothing. They just go back and forth without any kind of scrutiny.

Can you define for me or discuss how the U.S. Government defines special interest aliens? How do you do that?

Mr. BERSIN. If I might, I would ask Mr. Gonzalez or Mr. Kubiak to add. There are actually different definitions in part, depending on different agencies, but they all tend to be outside the Western Hemisphere. They tend to be either a listing of countries. I have seen listings up to 35 countries. Other agencies take up a more restricted terrorist-related or a terrorist-centric view of the definition. But I take your point.

We have no standard definition of special interest aliens, but I will tell you that consistent with Mr. Kubiak's point, when it comes to the checks that DHS personnel are making in Panama and Mexico, we take the biometrics of every person who is from outside the hemisphere so that we can check them against the holdings of the United States Government.

Mr. SIRES. Because I am thinking we were in Costa Rica. We went with the President and obviously, Costa Rica is going through this issue with the Cubans and the Costa Rica Government coming through, but only 60 percent of those people going through there are Cubans. They said 40 percent were basically other nationalities, from Africa, from Bangladesh, Pakistan. Do you determine—how do you determine there which ones are of special interest to us?

Mr. BERSIN. First, Mr. Sires, with due respect, I was corrected recently in preparation for the hearing on the proportion of special interest aliens. In fact, the large majority of people who are coming up from Panama into Costa Rica are actually Cubans. Three quarters of the flows are actually Cubans at this juncture and the number of special interest aliens from outside the hemisphere are actually a relatively smaller percentage. And a small number in terms of we are talking about 4,000 or 5,000.

Mr. SIRES. In my view, a smaller number is easier to get through our borders because you tend to pile them up together with the other people.

Mr. BERSIN. So in fact, having visited, then in fact, I would urge because I agree with Mr. Gonzalez and the chairman and you, Ranking Member, that visiting the five border areas is an eye opener and an important insight for American public servants, legislators, and Executive Branch alike, I suggest that you consider going down to Meteti in the Darien in Panama to view the work that is being done by HSI and Customs and Border Protection in concert with the American Embassy and Ambassador John Feeley in Panama.

It is interesting, but the arrangement we have there, Mr. Sires, is that we stop people, the Panamanians stop, detain people, for 7 or 10 days or longer depending on whether or not they come from a particular country, so that we can actually take their fingerprints and then check them so that, in fact, we can identify any high-risk persons coming through. But most of those people coming up through Panama are not special interest aliens.

Mr. SIRES. But you know my concern, right? Sometimes they get bundled in with the rest. But you said, did I hear you correctly? You said special interest aliens, you have one set of definitions, you have another set of definitions. There is no one set definition.

Mr. GONZALEZ. So Congressman, I think first to your other question, if I may, sir, I think part of the migration issue that we are facing, and Mr. Kubiak has some excellent examples of, we are cooperating with DHS and HSI to address the issues. Regardless of the definition of special interest aliens, in some regards, the flows that are coming through are ones that are taking up bandwidth for border officials, right? And a lot of this is a result of what I would say is less than strict immigration standards in some of these countries that actually led to what you saw as the almost 8,000 Cubans that ended up stuck in Costa Rica.

So one of the things that we have been doing is working with Costa Rica, Panama, and Colombia and even Ecuador to try to get them to implement stricter visa standards to actually stamp the passports so that when they are traveling through, in some of these countries, Costa Rica, for example, by law has to deport an immigrant to the country they were just in, but if their passport is not stamped, it makes it complicated because they don't actually show what their travel route is.

So we are actually working with them on the kind of reforms that they have to undertake. But then when they actually are—there are third country nationals that are in the country, what we will do is we will work with DHS and others to try to see if there is anybody of interest in that group that we need to actually—that poses a law enforcement challenge. And we can dive into this in the classified briefing to a certain extent, but it has been a two-pronged approach.

And to your question, sir, just on the special interest aliens is DoD has a larger definition than the State Department does and a lot of it has to do with where the—I think our number is either 38—36 or 38, and I can confirm that. And DoD has a 39 number. DHS has a more expansive number. And a lot of it has to do with countries that you see as posing a risk. So I think DHS poses a wider net because of the migration issues that they, of course, are working on.

Mr. KUBIAK. Sir, it is exactly your question for the reason I didn't use special interest alien in my opening statement because we are trying to get away from that term, specific terminology, because of this inherent problem that you have just identified. What we are referring to is third country nationals not from the Western Hemisphere, in other words, people from outside of our regional world. And it is specific because we are not necessarily worried about specific nationalities although there is some higher threat in certain areas of the world.

What we are worried about are bad actors within those communities, to your point exactly, and it is the ones and twos along the way that may have some intentional bad harm that we need to ferret out as Mr. Bersin said, shrink the haystack to make sure that we have really the best information possible about those that intend harm to the United States or to the region. And so it is programs like bitmap and our Transnational Criminal Investigative Units that we have worked in partnership with the other government agencies that allow us, and in the classified setting, I will get into much more detail in a couple of examples to give you how this exactly is working, but we are able to identify individuals to collect biometrics long before they get to the United States. Mr. Bersin did hint at even in some cases when we are able to do that, we are not able to then stop their forward and onward progression to the United States where they can show up at a port of entry and claim some form of relief.

Mr. SIRES. I have other questions, but we will get to it later. Thank you, Mr. Chairman.

Mr. DUNCAN. Mr. Yoho.

Mr. YOHO. Thank you, Mr. Chairman, and I appreciate all of you being here. Mr. Bersin, I appreciate the briefing before we went down to South America. It was a great trip. And I thought it was interesting when we were talking about the border security there in the tri-border area how they were telling us how lax it was, but when we met with some of the dignitaries, they said oh, no, we have got good border security. I saw a disconnect there.

I think we are all in agreement that border security is a national security issue. That is something we all take seriously. Obviously, you do, but yet we see the lapses, and I appreciate the work that you guys have done from the 1990s to today, but it is a different game today. Back then, we were worried more about people coming into this country wanting jobs, wanting a better life, wanting opportunity and the drug trafficking. Today, we have got people that want to do us harm and it is like a cake. You only need one drop of kerosene to mess up the whole batter and we can't afford any of that. And certainly we have seen that in what is going on in the European Union with Brussels, with Paris, with these attacks that like you said, is going to shut down our whole economy. It is their 9/11. Can we afford another one? Or do we want another one of those here in the United States?

And you are talking about the control. Before 9/11, we were pretty lax. 9/11 taught us a lesson. Now we have got TSA. Now we are doing checks at the curb, more perimeter checks before they even get into the airport. Where do we go next? Do the people just—five miles out from the airport? Or is it people coming into the cities, the people coming into a state? At what point do we say enough is enough and really crack down or find a different way to crack down?

Border security to me is a national security issue that has to be done. And I disagree with Mr. Trump wanting to build a wall. I don't think we need that. I think we have the technology, the personnel, and resources that we can do a good job, but it can't be done by itself. It has to be done with enforcement of the laws already on the book. Because right now there is a global policy around the world. People say there is a magnet, it is a global policy of unenforcement of immigration laws, that if you get to this area you get in and you get your pass go card, pass jail free card. It is the lottery for so many people. And they are struggling to do whatever they can to get here and if we can change some things and this is what I would like to hear from you guys.

Mr. Kubiak, you were talking about what you guys are doing on immigration and customs. I visited the Jacksonville Custom and Border Patrol people and they gave me several cases of where people were picked up. They took them back, put them on the plane to Honduras. A week later, they see them on I-10 driving by the same guy that deported them and the guy is smiling at our Custom and Border Patrol agent and it happens over and over again. They had several cases they showed me of convicted felons, whether it was DUIs or whether it was drugs or robbery that were deported, but they are back in this country because there is a revolving door. Plus, we were told there were directives coming out of the DHS and out of the White House and it was called PEP, the Presidential Enforcement Preference, where they are not enforcing or being told to let these people go.

So we can do all the right things and I commend the Custom and Border Patrol agents. They are doing the right thing, but when you have policies that are counter-productive, it is putting American lives at risk. All we have to do is look at the story of Kate Steinle, the young lady that was murdered out in San Francisco in a sanctuary city. We are working on defunding those kinds of cities, but not holding these people accountable and not allowing them back in. And when they are brought back in, they either need to be incarcerated or they need to make sure their host country keeps them in there.

We just saw what happened over the weekend in the Farmington neighborhood up here in Maryland where four people, three of them I think had already been deported one or two times, they are back in this area, causing crimes on American citizens. This is something that until we change, have a paradigm shift in how we deal with this. It is going to continue, and then God forbid that terrorist comes in illegally that should have been stopped, like you brought up in Honduras that didn't make it into Texas, luckily four of them got picked up. Was there one that didn't get picked up?

So they picked the one up, but how many have come through that haven't been picked up?

So what would you do, what would you recommend to us and I heard you, Mr. Bersin, say that until we change how these other countries deal with the people that were picked up and how we can deport them, what needs to change on this end to force those countries to do that? Is it withholding foreign aid? It is changing laws on our books? I would like to hear from both of you on that, what we need to do here to put an end to this because right now I see a revolving door on too many things and it is just a matter of time before somebody comes in and we have a problem.

Mr. KUBIAK. Thank you, sir. Thank you for the questions and for the opportunity to address. So just to answer your question first, the last question first, part of what I am seeing and that I mentioned in the opening statement to a degree is as you mentioned in the 1990s, prior to 9/11, we had different border strategy and we have changed that a lot over time. What I am seeing through our international partnership and engagement with our foreign counterparts and through our collaboration with State Department is that that is changing as well down in Central America, South America, and Mexico.

Specifically, in Mexico, we have seen an increased engagement over the last 2 years unlike I have ever seen before where they are attempting to address and they have a long way to go like we did pre-9/11 to the situation that we are today. But I think one of the things that we can do from here is a continued and constant capability building. We are never going to be able to enforce our way out of the illegal immigration floor solely. We have to have some impact on what we refer to as the push and pull factors that cause immigration. And so as you know, I am sure from your visit, a lot of the push factors are involved with reducing violence in the countries from which people are coming, Syria being the most tragic example, I think, and what is driving people out of that country. To continue to grow their economies so that we don't get as many economic migrants moving this way, and then to also work on reducing, as Mr. Bersin said, some of the immigration challenges that we have in the United States and some of the loopholes that we are able to address.

Mr. YOHO. Well, just along that line, the "ag" guest worker program, the H-1B visa, we have got farmers in our district that are going through the right process, they are recruiting the worker, they are going through the visa process. They get them into the United States. The workers know that the rules aren't going to be enforced, so they leave that farm and go into a different field of operation. Our farmers are calling ICE and ICE says nothing we can do. Those policies need to change on this end because it will put a stop on the change of people coming over here. And until we do that, people are just saying hey, get to America, they are not going to enforce that. Don't worry about it.

Those are the things that I want to see changed. And what do you need to do in your agency, who is preventing you from enforcing those laws on the book? Is it a directive coming out the White House?

Mr. KUBIAK. Sir, nobody is preventing us. We have resources. The priorities have been set by the Secretary.

Mr. YOHO. Secretary of?

Mr. KUBIAK. Secretary Johnson.

Mr. YOHO. Okay.

Mr. KUBIAK. Department of Homeland Security, that outlines the way that immigration——

Mr. YOHO. Why would they allow people to leave those H-1B visa that the farmer goes through to accomplish to get that person here legally? Why would they allow that not to be enforced?

Mr. KUBIAK. Sir, I am not——

Mr. YOHO. I'm sorry, it is H2-A visa.

Mr. KUBIAK. Yes, I apologize. I am not familiar specifically with that particular issue. I did spend some time as a special agent in charge in Northern New York where I worked with the U.S. Attorney's Office and we did do work in that——

Mr. YOHO. Those are the things that if we can change them and enforce it, it would stop that magnet and that pool of people saying, hey, don't worry about it, man. They are slack on that. They are not going to do anything. And then you are going to get this—the radical jihadist terrorist that is going to come through on a work visa and they are going to come in that way and that is—you know, I want to know who is going to be held accountable for that, what agency, what department? Who is going to answer to the kids, to the family, or the parents that got damaged in that attack? Yes, we should have enforced those laws, but we didn't. We are all going to have to answer to that and I don't want to answer that.

Let us see. And then the other thing that was brought up when I was visiting there, there was 1200 miles of coastline in Florida. We have 90 CBP, Custom Border Patrol agents, 70 boots on the ground. They did 4,000 arrests in the State of Florida or in that whole district. And they need more agents is what I was told, but there is some Northeast states that have 400 agents and they do 50 arrests a year. And is there a way to adjust those for need?

Mr. BERSIN. I am probably best equipped to respond to that. So the allocation formulas by region, Mr. Yoho, depend on a variety of factors. Arrests are one, but you could imagine a colleague in Vermont or Michigan, North Dakota, South Dakota that would still be concerned about having a sufficient number of agents there to patrol the territory they are responsible for.

So arrests are one, but not—I think CBP and Commissioner Kerlikowske can speak or Deputy McAleenan more directly to current practice. There is a pretty sophisticated workforce allocation model that takes into account a variety of matters which accounts, frankly, for the fact that of the 22,000 Border Patrol agents, 19,000 are in the 6 states—the 4 states of the Southwest border.

If I might though, address two issues on what we could be doing abroad. So when, in fact, the CBP and HSI officers in Panama and Meteti are running against special interest aliens or third country nationals, there is no capacity of the Panamanians right now to hold and detain large numbers. And the problem that we run into all the way up toward the Southwest border is that we often have trouble getting travel documents to be able to deport and to assist. There is no funding to support Panama or the Central American countries to do their own deportations in a systematic way. As we know from our experience, it takes a system to actually apprehend, detain, care for, and then deport a person who has no lawful right to be in a particular country. The Central American countries are at the very threshold of being able to develop that. But it would help, actually, and I could go into specifics with you and I would be happy to do it offline. There are a number of authorities at DRO that ICE does not have acting abroad that would permit it to actually assist in the deportation of people other than from the United States.

The second point, I have to go back and remind you that we have 243 Immigration Judges in this country, and we have 2000 Federal Judges. You cannot get the job done in a lawful, speedy, secure way with the paucity of resources. And when President Obama in 2014 asked the Congress for the resources to build an Immigration Court, we know what happened to that bill. The problems we have to address internally as well as abroad, sir. I grant you that premise.

Mr. DUNCAN. We will stand in recess. We will reconvene in the SCIF after votes.

[Whereupon, at 2:56 p.m., the subcommittee was adjourned.]

APPENDIX

_____

MATERIAL SUBMITTED FOR THE RECORD

SUBCOMMITTEE HEARING NOTICE
COMMITTEE ON FOREIGN AFFAIRS
U.S. HOUSE OF REPRESENTATIVES
WASHINGTON, DC 20515-6128

Subcommittee on the Western Hemisphere
Jeff Duncan (R-SC), Chairman

TO: MEMBERS OF THE COMMITTEE ON FOREIGN AFFAIRS

You are respectfully requested to attend an OPEN hearing of the Committee on Foreign Affairs, to be held by the Subcommittee on the Western Hemisphere in Room 2200 of the Rayburn House Office Building (and available live on the Committee website at http://www.ForeignAffairs.house.gov):

DATE: Tuesday, March 22, 2016

TIME: 2:00 p.m.

SUBJECT: Potential Terrorist Threats: Border Security Challenges in Latin America and the Caribbean

WITNESSES: Mr. Juan Gonzalez
                   Deputy Assistant Secretary
                   Bureau of Western Hemisphere Affairs
                   U.S. Department of State

                   The Honorable Alan D. Bersin
                   Assistant Secretary for International Affairs and Chief Diplomatic Officer
                   U.S. Department of Homeland Security

                   Mr. Lev Kubiak
                   Assistant Director for International Operations
                   U.S. Immigration and Customs Enforcement
                   U.S. Department of Homeland Security

By Direction of the Chairman

The Committee on Foreign Affairs seeks to make its facilities accessible to persons with disabilities. If you are in need of special accommodations, please call 202/225-5021 at least four business days in advance of the event, whenever practicable. Questions with regard to special accommodations in general (including availability of Committee materials in alternative formats and assistive listening devices) may be directed to the Committee.

COMMITTEE ON FOREIGN AFFAIRS

MINUTES OF SUBCOMMITTEE ON _____ *the Western Hemisphere* _____ HEARING

Day ____ *Tuesday* ____ Date _____ *03-22-2016* _____ Room _____ *2200* _____

Starting Time ____ *2:00 PM* ____ Ending Time ____ *02:56 PM* ____

Recesses | *n/a* | (____ to ____) (____ to ____) (____ to ____) (____ to ____) (____ to ____) (____ to ____)

Presiding Member(s)

Chairman Jeff Duncan

Check all of the following that apply:

Open Session ☑
Executive (closed) Session ☐
Televised ☑

Electronically Recorded (taped) ☑
Stenographic Record ☑

TITLE OF HEARING:

Potential Terrorist Threats: Border Security Challenges in Latin America and the Caribbean

SUBCOMMITTEE MEMBERS PRESENT:

Chairman Jeff Duncan, Ranking Member Albio Sires, Rep. Ted Yoho

NON-SUBCOMMITTEE MEMBERS PRESENT: *(Mark with an * if they are not members of full committee.)*

n/a

HEARING WITNESSES: Same as meeting notice attached? Yes ☑ No ☐
(If "no", please list below and include title, agency, department, or organization.)

STATEMENTS FOR THE RECORD: *(List any statements submitted for the record.)*

Chairman Jeff Duncan Opening Statement
Ranking Member Albio Sires Opening Statement

TIME SCHEDULED TO RECONVENE _____
or
TIME ADJOURNED ____ *02:56 PM* ____

Subcommittee Staff Director

Chairman Jeff Duncan
Opening Remarks
Foreign Affairs Committee's Subcommittee on the Western Hemisphere
"Potential Terrorist Threats: Border Security Challenges in Latin America and
the Caribbean"
Tuesday, March 22 at 2:00 p.m. in Rayburn Room 2200

I am deeply saddened by the loss of precious life this morning in Brussels at the hands of evil men, and I want to dedicate this hearing to the victims of today's attacks and their families. I led my very first Congressional delegation to Brussels to examine the foreign fighter threat and ways the U.S. and our European allies could better cooperate on homeland security issues. Only days before my visit, an ISIS foreign fighter had opened fire at the Jewish Museum of Belgium. Today's depraved acts in Brussels following so soon after last year's terrorist attack in Paris once again demonstrate evil men's intentions to rip apart the fabric of free Western societies by fear.

Such acts bring to mind Winston Churchill's words in May 1945: "Let us learn our lessons. Never, never, never believe any war will be smooth and easy . . . Always remember, however sure you are that you can easily win, that there would not be a war if the other man did not think he also had a chance." We must show our enemies that they have no chance of victory, and we do that, in part, through strong defenses and secure borders. In today's hearing, I want to examine potential terrorist threats to the U.S. and to countries in the Western Hemisphere from border security vulnerabilities in the region. Following last November's terrorist attack in Paris, reports surfaced that a Syrian individual under investigation for participating in the attacks had traveled to Brazil, Ecuador, and Colombia in July before allegedly bribing a Colombian official to leave the country.

In the past few months, Costa Rica, Honduras, St. Maarten, Panama, and Paraguay have all apprehended several Syrians attempting to reach the United States. In one particular case last November, five Syrians who were apprehended by Honduran authorities had reportedly bought fake passports in Brazil and traveled freely through Argentina and Costa Rica without being stopped. These issues caught my attention, and as Chairman of this Subcommittee, I led a bipartisan Congressional delegation to several countries in the region to better understand the security situation and to see first-hand what challenges countries face and how they are working to address them. While I was encouraged by the efforts of the governments in Argentina and Paraguay to prioritize border security and counternarcotics issues, I was concerned to learn of an influx of migration from Syrian nationals and other "special interest aliens" (SIAs), people from countries that have active terrorism cells or networks, who are using fraudulent passports in Latin America.

Furthermore, Commander Tidd of U.S. Southern Command (SOUTHCOM) testified to the U.S. Congress earlier this month that in each of the cases where Latin American or Caribbean partner nations detained groups of Syrians, "access to fraudulent or stolen documents and corrupt law enforcement officials facilitated SIA movement through numerous countries." Corruption is a huge problem, and bad actors are experts at exploiting it. In addition to the increase in Syrian travelers, Mexico's Interior Ministry recorded a 90 percent increase in African apprehensions and a 180 percent increase in Asian apprehensions last year compared to 2014 of individuals from Eritrea, Pakistan, and Somalia. Ultimately, last November, three groups of people from Syria, Pakistan, and Afghanistan reportedly tried to enter the U.S. through our Southern border.

While there's certainly a place for legitimate travel, this uptick in travel from SIAs who are aiming to reach the United States is concerning. After all, Interpol stated last November that of the estimated 25,000 foreign terrorist combatants thought to be operating across the globe, only 5,600 have been identified by law enforcement agencies. This means we have almost 20,000 foreign fighters that no one has identified. When we add to this huge intelligence blind spot countries in the Western Hemisphere with lax border controls: limited capacity to detect forged documents; corrupt border officials; areas where borders are largely ungoverned or that have criminal networks, such as the Darién in Panama and the Tri-Border Area of Paraguay, Argentina, and Brazil; we need to recognize that our hemisphere has a monumental challenge in identifying threats and preventing foreign fighter travel.

Today, South America's leading trade bloc, Mercosur, and Central America's C-4 Agreement allow visa-free travel similar to the Schengen Area in Europe. Five Caribbean countries have also established Citizen-by-Investment Programs (CIPs) that offer fast-track citizenship and create the potential for fraud and corruption. In 2014, the U.S. Department of Treasury's Financial Crimes Enforcement Network (FinCEN) issued an advisory to financial institutions that Iranian nationals were abusing the CIPs to engage in illicit activities. This challenging security environment presents clear risks to the United States and to countries in the region, which is one reason I authored legislation called the Countering Iran in the Western Hemisphere Act, which became U.S. law in 2012.

This legislation was meant to address Congressional concerns about Iranian and Hezbollah's activities in the region by requiring a threat assessment and strategy to address it. In September 2014, the Government Accountability Office (GAO) found that the U.S. Department of State's strategy for countering Iranian influence in the Western Hemisphere only fully addressed two of the 12 elements identified in the law, and GAO recommended that State provide Congress with information to fully address these elements. I am interested in hearing more from State on this issue, especially as it relates to the border security strategy requirements in the law and any extra measures Latin American and Caribbean countries are now taking in view of recent events.

Moreover, I am also concerned about young recruits from Latin America and the Caribbean going to join ISIS in Syria. Last year, the former Commander of SOUTHCOM named Jamaica, Suriname, and Trinidad and Tobago as having had citizens leave for Syria. This year, SOUTHCOM disclosed to Congress that many of the countries in the Western Hemisphere "are unable to monitor the potential return of foreign fighters and often lack robust counterterrorism legislation and capabilities to confront this threat."

In conclusion, today's terrorist attacks in Brussels and last year's attack in Paris should galvanize us into action. No country is immune to attacks from foreign fighters. Unfortunately, the Western Hemisphere with its porous borders, free-trade zones, and corruption problems is ripe for exploitation by those who wish to do us harm. It is my hope that countries in the region will recognize this and work to deepen cooperation. U.S. technology and equipment alone will not make the region safer: we need better information-sharing, tighter and systematic ID checks in the region, and stronger border security measures, including regular vetting for corruption within customs' agencies. With that, I turn to Ranking Member Sires for his opening statement.

House Committee on Foreign Affairs **Congressman Albio Sires (D-NJ)**
Subcommittee on the Western Hemisphere **Ranking Member**

Opening Statement - "Potential Terrorist Threats: Border Security Challenges in Latin America
& the Caribbean""
Tuesday, March 22, 2016

− Thank you Mr. Chairman. Good afternoon and thank you to our witnesses for being here.

− Today we are examining potential threats to the United States and countries in the Western Hemisphere from border security vulnerabilities in the region.

− This hearing comes at a particularly important time as the Chairman and I have just returned from a CoDel to South and Central America where we specifically examined these border security challenges.

− Since the attacks on September 11th and the more recent November 2015 Paris attacks, many have expressed concerns that terrorists might infiltrate the United States through the Southwest border.

− While the vast-majority of individuals apprehended at the U-S - Mexico border over the years have come from Central America, Cuba, or other countries in the region, recently, U-S authorities have increasingly apprehended individuals from Africa, Asia, and the Middle East.

− Some of those apprehended have originated in "special interest" countries, including Pakistan, Afghanistan, Nigeria and Somalia, which have active terrorist networks operating within their territories.

− Smuggling rings charge desperate migrants thousands of dollars to guide them through long and dangerous routes that involve entering the Western Hemisphere via air through Brazil, Ecuador, or Cuba or traveling by bus, air, or boat to Central America;

− Then, the migrants follow operatives who pay off drug traffickers and corrupt border officials and lead them through the region.

House Committee on Foreign Affairs
Subcommittee on the Western Hemisphere

Congressman Albio Sires (D-NJ)
Ranking Member

Opening Statement - "Potential Terrorist Threats: Border Security Challenges in Latin America & the Caribbean""
Tuesday, March 22, 2016

- Travel from Africa, Asia, or the Middle East to Mexico often takes at least several months if not years.

- There are documented incidents where individuals traveling illegally from the Middle East on false passports have successfully passed through several Latin American countries before being apprehended.

- Most notably, last November five Syrians were apprehended by Honduran authorities traveling on fake passports reportedly bought in Brazil.

- These individuals got through the border controls of Argentina and Costa Rica before they were caught in Honduras.

- Even though these individuals were shown to not have any militant links, this incident pointed real concerns about the region's border security.

- Many countries in Latin America have limited funding and capacity to patrol their long and often sparsely populated borders, and to rigorously screen individuals at their respective ports of entry.

- This lack of rigorous vetting and the internal controls necessary to root out corruption within the immigration agencies of several of our hemispheric allies is a serious threat to the security of our homeland.

- The U-S provides millions of dollars in assistance to support robust security initiatives that include components of border security.

- These include the Merida Initiative with Mexico, the Caribbean Basin Security Initiative, and the Central America Regional Security Initiative.

House Committee on Foreign Affairs
Subcommittee on the Western Hemisphere

Congressman Albio Sires (D-NJ)
Ranking Member

Opening Statement - "Potential Terrorist Threats: Border Security Challenges in Latin America & the Caribbean""
Tuesday, March 22, 2016

- I believe we should ensure that some of these funds go towards addressing these threats.

- I look forward to hearing from our witnesses about these initiatives and other U-S regional efforts regarding border security. Thank you

www.ingramcontent.com/pod-product-compliance
Lightning Source LLC
Chambersburg PA
CBHW081755280526
45789CB00008B/2862